McCaulay's Maryland Real Estate Licensing Exams State Portion Sample Exams and Study Guide

By Philip Martin McCaulay

National Harbor, Maryland

The Maryland Real Estate Licensing Commission does not endorse, promote, review, or warrant the accuracy of products or services offered by Philip Martin McCaulay. Philip Martin McCaulay is not affiliated with the Maryland Real Estate Licensing Commission.

McCaulay's Maryland Real Estate Licensing Exams
State Portion Sample Exams and Study Guide

Published in Raleigh, North Carolina, USA
978-0-557-72782-7

Preface

McCaulay's Maryland Real Estate Licensing Exams State Portion Sample Exams and Study Guide includes four complete 30-question sample exams for the Maryland State portion of the real estate licensing exam, for a total of 120 practice questions. Each 30-question practice exam is followed by the answer key and a copy of the exam with the answers shown. After the sample exams, there is a complete study guide in outline form covering all of the topics found on the Maryland State portion of the exam, including the duties and powers of the Real Estate Commission, licensing requirements, and business conduct.

Study time should be allocated in proportion to the weight of the material on the actual exam. Focus on the material most likely to be on the exam.

Maryland Real Estate Salesperson Exam Topic	Number of Questions
Duties and Powers of the Real Estate Commission	4
Licensing Requirements	4
Business Conduct	22
Total	30

The best way to prepare is to take practice exams that are in the same format as the actual exam and test the material in the same proportion. Taking practice exams will identify the areas that need to be improved. Focus on studying the areas that need improvement, and then take more practice exams.

When taking a multiple choice exam with four possible answers, usually one answer can be eliminated instantly, and another answer can be eliminated with a little knowledge of the subject. It usually comes down to choosing between the two best possible answers.

About half the questions will be relatively easy and the other half will be more challenging. Try to make sure you get the easy half correct. Narrow the choices for the more difficult questions to two choices, and pick the best one. Getting all the easy questions correct and guessing correctly on about half of the more difficult questions should result in a passing score.

There is no penalty for a wrong answer, so do not leave any questions blank. Do not spend too much time on any one question. If a question is challenging, eliminate one or two or the choices, make your best guess from the remaining possible answers, and move on. Keep track of the time to make sure you complete all of the questions and allow for time to go back and review the answers.

Table of Contents

Table of Contents (continued)

Sample Exam 1

1. The Maryland Real Estate Commission has

    A. 7 licensed members

    B. 9 licensed members

    C. 4 licensed members and 5 unlicensed members

    D. 5 licensed members and 4 unlicensed members

2. Prior to a hearing, a licensee being investigated gets at least

    A. 3 days notice

    B. 10 days notice

    C. 20 days notice

    D. 30 days notice

3. What is the maximum amount that can be recovered from the Guaranty Fund?

    A. $5,000

    B. $25,000

    C. $50,000

    D. $250,000

4. After a payment is made from the Guaranty Fund, what action is taken against the licensee causing the claim?

    A. Hold a hearing

    B. Immediate license suspension

    C. Advise the supervising broker

    D. Post notice in the Maryland Register for 90 days

5. An unlicensed employee may not

    A. Assemble documents for closing

    B. Secure documents from the courthouse

    C. Discuss a contract outside the brokerage

    D. Follow up on loan commitments

6. Expired licenses may be reinstated within

    A. 4 years of expiration

    B. 5 years of expiration

    C. 7 years of expiration

    D. 10 years of expiration

7. How many continuing education hours must be on the topic of Ethics, Flipping, and Predatory Lending?

   A. 1.5 hours

   B. 3 hours

   C. 7.5 hours

   D. 9 hours

8. Who would be required to hold a license?

   A. Bank selling foreclosures

   B. Homebuilder selling new homes

   C. Lawyer engaged in real estate brokerage

   D. Owner subdividing six unimproved lots

9. What action should a licensee take after receiving an offer on a property under contract?

   A. Do not present the offer

   B. Do not present the offer unless it is better

   C. Present the offer within 30 days

   D. Present the offer in a timely manner

10. Which would require an appraisal rather than a CMA?

    A.   An estate settlement

    B.   Assisting in the deciding the sale price

    C.   Assisting in the deciding the buying price

    D.   Assisting in the deciding the offering price

11. Records of trust money must be

    A. Filed with the Commission

    B. Posted on the Maryland Register

    C. Kept in a secure area of the broker's office

    D. Kept in a safety deposit box at a financial
institution

12. Referral fees

    A.   May never be paid

    B.   May not be paid to unlicensed persons

    C.   Are set by negotiation with unlicensed persons

    D.   May not be paid as a percentage

13. A licensee must disclose knowledge of

    A. A death on a property

    B. A felony on a property

    C. A property owner having AIDS

    D. Hidden defects

14. A broker providing evidence of reasonable and
    adequate supervision would produce evidence of

    A. Legal opinion on all executed contracts

    B. Conducting training meetings

    C. Review of all advertisements placed by affiliate

    D. Review of affiliate's credit report

15. Prior to changing the location of an office or escrow
    account, a broker must give the Commission

    A. 7 days notice

    B. 10 days notice

    C. 15 days notice

    D. 30 days notice

16. Which type of agent represents only the seller?

    A. Dual agent

    B. Intra-company agent

    C. Cooperating agent

    D. Presumed buyer's agent

17. The Brokers Act requires that the form Understanding
    Whom Agents Represent be presented not later than

    A. Closing

    B. The day an agreement is signed

    C. The first scheduled face-to-face meeting

    D. 10 days after the first scheduled meeting

18. Unless a property is listed by an agent or the agent's
    broker, the agent is assumed to be acting on behalf of
    the

    A. Buyer

    B. Seller

    C. Broker

    D. Agent

19. Which practice is legal in Maryland?

    A. Blockbusting

    B. Net listings

    C. Automatic extensions

    D. Ground rents

20. Who has the right to choose the buyer's settlement attorney, escrow agent, and title company?

    A. Buyer

    B. Licensee

    C. Seller

    D. Broker

21. Salespersons and associate brokers licenses must be

    A. Displayed in the broker's branch office

    B. Filed with the Secretary of State

    C. Filed with the Attorney General

    D. Filed with the Real Estate Commission

22. Client's money must be deposited by the broker or
the broker's designee in the firm's trust account within

    A. 6 days

    B. 9 days

    C. 5 business days

    D. 7 business days

23. All Team advertising must contain

    A. The name of at least two licensed Team members

    B. The fax number of the broker or branch manager

    C. The nickname of the team

    D. The full name of the brokerage displayed in a
meaningful and conspicuous manner

24. Listing contracts are with the

    A. Brokers not the salesperson

    B. Salesperson not the broker

    C. Buyer and seller

    D. Seller and the MLS

25. Ways licensees must gather material facts include

    A. Hiring an appraiser

    B. Having the buyer complete disclosure forms

    C. Inspecting the property

    D. Complying with Regulation Z

26. Nonresidential property does not include

    A. Commercial or industrial property

    B. Property zoned for agricultural use

    C. Unimproved property zoned for multifamily units

    D. Property improved by five or more single-family units

27. A right of cancellation is given to a purchaser of a new timeshare for

    A.   10 days

    B.   12 days

    C.   15 days

    D.   30 days

28. Regarding Evidence of Title in Maryland,

    A. A Torrens Certificate is required

    B. A buyer is responsible for securing evidence of title

    C. A Quitclaim Deed is required

    D. A seller is responsible for securing evidence of title

29. Regarding security deposits in Maryland,

    A. The maximum is 3 months rent

    B. Interest on security deposits accrues every six months and does not compound

    C. Deposits must be returned within 90 days

    D. They are illegal on percentage leases

30. The Maryland Lead Poisoning Prevention Program

    A. Is mandatory for all units built before 1974

    B. Pays for relocation and medical expenses

    C. Introduced innocent landowner liability

    D. Applies to underground storage tanks

Sample Exam 1 Answer Key

1. D

2. B

3. B

4. B

5. C

6. A

7. B

8. C

9. D

10. A

11. C

12. B

13. D

14. C

15. A

16. C

17. C

18. A

19. D

20. A

21. A

22. D

23. D

24. A

25. C

26. B

27. A

28. B

29. B

30. B

Sample Exam 1 with Answers Shown

1. The Maryland Real Estate Commission has

   A. 7 licensed members

   B. 9 licensed members

   C. 4 licensed members and 5 unlicensed members

   *D. 5 licensed members and 4 unlicensed members

2. Prior to a hearing, a licensee being investigated gets at least

   A. 3 days notice

   *B. 10 days notice

   C. 20 days notice

   D. 30 days notice

3. What is the maximum amount that can be recovered from the Guaranty Fund?

   A. $5,000

   *B. $25,000

   C. $50,000

   D. $250,000

4. After a payment is made from the Guaranty Fund, what action is taken against the licensee causing the claim?

    A. Hold a hearing

    *B. Immediate license suspension

    C. Advise the supervising broker

    D. Post notice in the Maryland Register for 90 days

5. An unlicensed employee may not

    A. Assemble documents for closing

    B. Secure documents from the courthouse

    *C. Discuss a contract outside the brokerage

    D. Follow up on loan commitments

6. Expired licenses may be reinstated within

    *A. 4 years of expiration

    B. 5 years of expiration

    C. 7 years of expiration

    D. 10 years of expiration

7. How many continuing education hours must be on the topic of Ethics, Flipping, and Predatory Lending?

    A. 1.5 hours

    *B. 3 hours

    C. 7.5 hours

    D. 9 hours

8. Who would be required to hold a license?

    A.   Bank selling foreclosures

    B.   Homebuilder selling new homes

    *C. Lawyer engaged in real estate brokerage

    D.   Owner subdividing six unimproved lots

9. What action should a licensee take after receiving an offer on a property under contract?

    A. Do not present the offer

    B. Do not present the offer unless it is better

    C. Present the offer within 30 days

    *D. Present the offer in a timely manner

10. Which would require an appraisal rather than a CMA?

   *A. An estate settlement

   B.   Assisting in the deciding the sale price

   C.   Assisting in the deciding the buying price

   D.   Assisting in the deciding the offering price

11. Records of trust money must be

   A.   Filed with the Commission

   B.   Posted on the Maryland Register

   *C. Kept in a secure area of the broker's office

   D.   Kept in a safety deposit box at a financial
        institution

12. Referral fees

   A.   May never be paid

   *B. May not be paid to unlicensed persons

   C.   Are set by negotiation with unlicensed persons

   D.   May not be paid as a percentage

13. A licensee must disclose knowledge of

    A.   A death on a property

    B.   A felony on a property

    C.   A property owner having AIDS

    *D. Hidden defects

14. A broker providing evidence of reasonable and adequate supervision would produce evidence of

    A.   Legal opinion on all executed contracts

    B.   Conducting training meetings

    *C. Review of all advertisements placed by affiliate

    D.   Review of affiliate's credit report

15. Prior to changing the location of an office or escrow account, a broker must give the Commission

    *A. 7 days notice

    B.   10 days notice

    C.   15 days notice

    D.   30 days notice

16. Which type of agent represents only the seller?

    A. Dual agent

    B. Intra-company agent

    *C. Cooperating agent

    D. Presumed buyer's agent

17. The Brokers Act requires that the form Understanding Whom Agents Represent be presented not later than

    A. Closing

    B. The day an agreement is signed

    *C. The first scheduled face-to-face meeting

    D. 10 days after the first scheduled meeting

18. Unless a property is listed by an agent or the agent's broker, the agent is assumed to be acting on behalf of the

    *A. Buyer

    B. Seller

    C. Broker

    D. Agent

19. Which practice is legal in Maryland?

    A. Blockbusting

    B. Net listings

    C. Automatic extensions

    *D. Ground rents

20. Who has the right to choose the buyer's settlement attorney, escrow agent, and title company?

    *A. Buyer

    B. Licensee

    C. Seller

    D. Broker

21. Salespersons and associate brokers licenses must be

    *A. Displayed in the broker's branch office

    B. Filed with the Secretary of State

    C. Filed with the Attorney General

    D. Filed with the Real Estate Commission

22. Client's money must be deposited by the broker or the broker's designee in the firm's trust account within

    A. 6 days

    B. 9 days

    C. 5 business days

    *D. 7 business days

23. All Team advertising must contain

    A. The name of at least two licensed Team members

    B. The fax number of the broker or branch manager

    C. The nickname of the team

    *D. The full name of the brokerage displayed in a meaningful and conspicuous manner

24. Listing contracts are with the

    *A. Brokers not the salesperson

    B. Salesperson not the broker

    C. Buyer and seller

    D. Seller and the MLS

25. Ways licensees must gather material facts include

    A. Hiring an appraiser

    B. Having the buyer complete disclosure forms

    *C. Inspecting the property

    D. Complying with Regulation Z

26. Nonresidential property does not include

    A. Commercial or industrial property

    *B. Property zoned for agricultural use

    C. Unimproved property zoned for multifamily units

    D. Property improved by five or more single-family units

27. A right of cancellation is given to a purchaser of a new timeshare for

    *A. 10 days

    B. 12 days

    C. 15 days

    D. 30 days

28. Regarding Evidence of Title in Maryland,

    A. A Torrens Certificate is required

    *B. A buyer is responsible for securing evidence of title

    C. A Quitclaim Deed is required

    D. A seller is responsible for securing evidence of title

29. Regarding security deposits in Maryland,

    A. The maximum is 3 months rent

    *B. Interest on security deposits accrues every six months and does not compound

    C. Deposits must be returned within 90 days

    D. They are illegal on percentage leases

30. The Maryland Lead Poisoning Prevention Program

    A. Is mandatory for all units built before 1974

    *B. Pays for relocation and medical expenses

    C. Introduced innocent landowner liability

    D. Applies to underground storage tanks

Sample Exam 2

1. Claims for payments from the Guaranty Fund

    A. Are not required to be in writing

    B. Must be for actual cash loss

    C. May be filed by the spouse of the individual responsible for the act

    D. Must be for discrimination

2. Which is a right of the Commission?

    A. To set redemption periods for foreclosures

    B. To take action against unlicensed individuals

    C. To amend, adopt, and repeal legislation

    D. To prohibit conspiracies that restrain trade

3. Prior to making changes to rules and regulations, the Commission must post the proposed changes on the

    A. Website for 45 days

    B. Website for 90 days

    C. Maryland Register for 45 days

    D. Maryland Register for 90 days

4. What are the maximum fines that the Commission is authorized to impose for the first three violations?

    A. $5,000, $10,000, and $15,000

    B. $5,000, $15,000, and $25,000

    C. $10,000, $15,000, and $25,000

    D. $10,000, $25,000, and $50,000

5. A license may be placed on inactive status for up to

    A. 4 years

    B. 5 years

    C. 7 years

    D. 10 years

6. The requirements for a broker's license include

    A. 60 hours of required education

    B. Three years of experience as a salesperson

    C. A credit score of at least 720

    D. Having lived in the area for at least five years

7. An unlicensed employee may

    A. Have keys made for company listings

    B. Be paid on the basis of real estate activity

    C. Discuss property attributes with a prospect

    D. Show property to a friend

8. To be licensed, applicants must

    A. Submit irrevocable consent

    B. Have lived in the area for three years

    C. Be affiliated with an appraiser

    D. Be professionally competent and of good character and reputation

9. Licensees must give copies of listing agreements to all parties

    A. Immediately

    B. In a timely manner

    C. Within 30 days

    D. Within 45 days

10. If a salesperson leaves a brokerage, the salesperson's listings

    A. Are terminated

    B. Stay with the brokerage

    C. Go with the salesperson

    D. Stay or go, depending on the client

11. A broker may not pay a commission to an unlicensed person with an exception for

    A. No one

    B. Lawyers

    C. Referral fees

    D. A broker licensed in another state

12. Placing a "for sale" sign on a property without permission from the owner is

    A. Unethical

    B. Steering

    C. Blockbusting

    D. Prejudicial solicitation

13. If a licensee receives two written offers on a property,

   A. The best offer should be presented first

   B. The offers should be presented in the order received

   C. Both offers must be presented within 24 hours

   D. Both offers must be presented in a timely manner

14. Automatic suspension of a broker's license could occur for

   A. Failing to provide notice of phone number change

   B. Failing to provide upon request all records concerning earnest money deposits

   C. Arrest for driving under the influence

   D. An affiliate failing to renew license

15. Which type of agent represents only the buyer?

   A. Presumed buyer's agent

   B. Intra-company agent

   C. Cooperating agent

   D. Dual agent

16. Broker's clients are their

   A.   Principals

   B.   Agents

   C.   Customers

   D.   Prospects

17. A customer could infer that an agency relationship exists based on

   A.   Payment or promise of payment

   B.   Performance of ministerial (servant) duties

   C.   Receipt of magisterial (expert) guidance

   D.   Pledge of property for security on a debt

18. The amount of brokerage agreed upon may be a

   A.   Net amount or a net percentage

   B.   Net amount or a specific percentage

   C.   Specific amount or a net percentage

   D.   Specific amount or a specific percentage

19. Based on the activity of a person who should have been properly licensed but was not, a firm can claim

   A. A full commission payable immediately

   B. A full commission payable at a later date

   C. A partial commission

   D. No commission

20. A licensee greeting customers at an open house must present "Understanding Whom Agents Represent"

   A. Immediately

   B. In a timely manner

   C. Within 30 days

   D. Not later than the first scheduled meeting

21. Required disclosures before the sales contract include

   A. CERCLA and Regulation Z

   B. Multiple listing agreement and buyer agency agreement

   C. Agency and seller condition disclaimer

   D. RESPA and Truth in Lending

22. Which is true regarding Teams and Groups?

    A. A licensed broker may be a member of a Team

    B. The name may include "Real Estate" or "Realty"

    C. Teams must conduct all real estate activities from the office where their license are displayed

    D. Teams may only offer exclusive agency listings

23. Regarding Teams or Groups and Dual Agency,

    A. The Team Leader may designate Team Members as intra-company agents

    B. Only the Broker may designate Team Members as intra-company agents

    C. Member of teams may not be fiduciaries

    D. Dual agents are special and general agents

24. Property transfers must be in writing except

    A. Ground leases

    B. Timeshares

    C. Short term leases

    D. Unimproved property

25. Which is a legal estate recognized in Maryland?

    A. Curtesy

    B. Dower

    C. Homestead

    D. Leasehold

26. The purchase price of a ground lease is the annual rent

    A. Divided by a factor in the range of 0.04 to 0.12

    B. Divided by a factor in the range of 0.27 to 0.54

    C. Multiplied by a factor in the range of 0.04 to 0.12

    D. Multiplied by a factor in the range of 0.27 to 0.54

27. A right of cancellation is given to a purchaser of a new condominium for

    A. 7 days

    B. 10 days

    C. 15 days

    D. 30 days

28. Which is most accurate regarding a Deed of Trust?

    A.   It is the security instrument preferred by
         Maryland lenders

    B.   It creates an involuntary lien

    C.   It diminishes the value of a property

    D.   It is the most complete type of ownership

29. Which is a prohibited provision in leases in Maryland?

    A.   Late penalty of more than 2%

    B.   Automatic renewal for longer than one month

    C.   A covenant for the tenant to restore the premises
         in good repair

    D.   Triple net lease

30. Which is most accurate regarding title insurance?

    A.   Lenders seldom require title insurance

    B.   State law requires that purchasers be offered
         homeowner's title insurance at closing

    C.   It allows buyers to borrow with a greater LTV

    D.   It is required under RESPA

Sample Exam 2 Answer Key

1. B

2. B

3. C

4. B

5. A

6. B

7. A

8. D

9. B

10. B

11. D

12. A

13. D

14. B

15. A

16. A

17. C

18. D

19. D

20. D

21. C

22. C

23. B

24. C

25. D

26. A

27. C

28. A

29. B

30. B

Sample Exam 2 with Answers Shown

1. Claims for payments from the Guaranty Fund

  A. Are not required to be in writing

  *B. Must be for actual cash loss

  C. May be filed by the spouse of the individual responsible for the act

  D. Must be for discrimination

2. Which is a right of the Commission?

  A. To set redemption periods for foreclosures

  *B. To take action against unlicensed individuals

  C. To amend, adopt, and repeal legislation

  D. To prohibit conspiracies that restrain trade

3. Prior to making changes to rules and regulations, the Commission must post the proposed changes on the

  A. Website for 45 days

  B. Website for 90 days

  *C. Maryland Register for 45 days

  D. Maryland Register for 90 days

4. What are the maximum fines that the Commission is authorized to impose for the first three violations?

    A. $5,000, $10,000, and $15,000

    *B. $5,000, $15,000, and $25,000

    C. $10,000, $15,000, and $25,000

    D. $10,000, $25,000, and $50,000

5. A license may be placed on inactive status for up to

    *A. 4 years

    B.   5 years

    C.   7 years

    D.   10 years

6. The requirements for a broker's license include

    A. 60 hours of required education

    *B. Three years of experience as a salesperson

    C. A credit score of at least 720

    D. Having lived in the area for at least five years

7. An unlicensed employee may

    *A. Have keys made for company listings

    B. Be paid on the basis of real estate activity

    C. Discuss property attributes with a prospect

    D. Show property to a friend

8. To be licensed, applicants must

    A. Submit irrevocable consent

    B. Have lived in the area for three years

    C. Be affiliated with an appraiser

    *D. Be professionally competent and of good
       character and reputation

9. Licensees must give copies of listing agreements to all
   parties

    A. Immediately

    *B. In a timely manner

    C. Within 30 days

    D. Within 45 days

10. If a salesperson leaves a brokerage, the salesperson's listings

    A. Are terminated

    *B. Stay with the brokerage

    C. Go with the salesperson

    D. Stay or go, depending on the client

11. A broker may not pay a commission to an unlicensed person with an exception for

    A. No one

    B. Lawyers

    C. Referral fees

    *D. A broker licensed in another state

12. Placing a "for sale" sign on a property without permission from the owner is

    *A. Unethical

    B. Steering

    C. Blockbusting

    D. Prejudicial solicitation

13. If a licensee receives two written offers on a property,

    A. The best offer should be presented first

    B. The offers should be presented in the order
        received

    C. Both offers must be presented within 24 hours

    *D. Both offers must be presented in a timely manner

14. Automatic suspension of a broker's license could
    occur for

    A. Failing to provide notice of phone number change

    *B. Failing to provide upon request all records
        concerning earnest money deposits

    C. Arrest for driving under the influence

    D. An affiliate failing to renew license

15. Which type of agent represents only the buyer?

    *A. Presumed buyer's agent

    B. Intra-company agent

    C. Cooperating agent

    D. Dual agent

16. Broker's clients are their

    *A. Principals

    B.   Agents

    C.   Customers

    D.   Prospects

17. A customer could infer that an agency relationship exists based on

    A.   Payment or promise of payment

    B.   Performance of ministerial (servant) duties

    *C. Receipt of magisterial (expert) guidance

    D.   Pledge of property for security on a debt

18. The amount of brokerage agreed upon may be a

    A.   Net amount or a net percentage

    B.   Net amount or a specific percentage

    C.   Specific amount or a net percentage

    *D. Specific amount or a specific percentage

19. Based on the activity of a person who should have been properly licensed but was not, a firm can claim

   A. A full commission payable immediately

   B. A full commission payable at a later date

   C. A partial commission

   *D. No commission

20. A licensee greeting customers at an open house must present "Understanding Whom Agents Represent"

   A. Immediately

   B. In a timely manner

   C. Within 30 days

   *D. Not later than the first scheduled meeting

21. Required disclosures before the sales contract include

   A. CERCLA and Regulation Z

   B. Multiple listing agreement and buyer agency agreement

   *C. Agency and seller condition disclaimer

   D. RESPA and Truth in Lending

22. Which is true regarding Teams and Groups?

    A. A licensed broker may be a member of a Team

    B. The name may include "Real Estate" or "Realty"

    *C. Teams must conduct all real estate activities from
        the office where their license are displayed

    D. Teams may only offer exclusive agency listings

23. Regarding Teams or Groups and Dual Agency,

    A. The Team Leader may designate Team Members
        as intra-company agents

    *B. Only the Broker may designate Team Members as
        intra-company agents

    C. Member of teams may not be fiduciaries

    D. Dual agents are special and general agents

24. Property transfers must be in writing except

    A. Ground leases

    B. Timeshares

    *C. Short term leases

    D. Unimproved property

25. Which is a legal estate recognized in Maryland?

    A. Curtesy

    B. Dower

    C. Homestead

    *D. Leasehold

26. The purchase price of a ground lease is the annual
    rent

    *A. Divided by a factor in the range of 0.04 to 0.12

    B. Divided by a factor in the range of 0.27 to 0.54

    C. Multiplied by a factor in the range of 0.04 to 0.12

    D. Multiplied by a factor in the range of 0.27 to 0.54

27. A right of cancellation is given to a purchaser of a new
    condominium for

    A. 7 days

    B. 10 days

    *C. 15 days

    D. 30 days

28. Which is most accurate regarding a Deed of Trust?

  *A. It is the security instrument preferred by
       Maryland lenders

  B.   It creates an involuntary lien

  C.   It diminishes the value of a property

  D.   It is the most complete type of ownership

29. Which is a prohibited provision in leases in Maryland?

  A.   Late penalty of more than 2%

  *B. Automatic renewal for longer than one month

  C.   A covenant for the tenant to restore the premises
       in good repair

  D.   Triple net lease

30. Which is most accurate regarding title insurance?

  A.   Lenders seldom require title insurance

  *B. State law requires that purchasers be offered
       homeowner's title insurance at closing

  C.   It allows buyers to borrow with a greater LTV

  D.   It is required under RESPA

Sample Exam 3

1. The Maryland Real Estate Commission licensed commissioners must have been licensed for at least

    A. 4 years

    B. 5 years

    C. 7 years

    D. 10 years

2. The minimum level of the Guaranty Fund is

    A. $25,000

    B. $250,000

    C. $2,500,000

    D. $25,000,000

3. Time to respond to the Commission for a claim against the Guaranty Fund is

    A. 3 days

    B. 10 days

    C. 20 days

    D. 30 days

4. Each Real Estate Hearing Board shall consist of at least three members of the Commission including

    A. The Chairperson

    B. The Executive Director

    C. At least two professional members

    D. At least one professional member and at least one consumer member

5. A licensee may become affiliated with more than one broker

    A. If each broker is given notice of the affiliations

    B. If one is outside the state

    C. With written permission from the Commission

    D. Under no circumstances

6. License renewal notices are mailed within

    A. 30 days of expiration

    B. 3 months of expiration

    C. 6 months of expiration

    D. 1 year of expiration

7. How many of the continuing education hours must be on the topic of Legislative Updates?

    A. 1.5 hours

    B. 3 hours

    C. 7.5 hours

    D. 9 hours

8. An unlicensed employee may

    A. Place signs on the property

    B. Conduct an open house

    C. Receive commission checks

    D. Collect deposit monies

9. A broker wishing to provide evidence of reasonable and adequate supervision would produce evidence of

    A. Commission checks

    B. The broker's legal opinion on executed contracts

    C. Compliance with the firm's written procedures

    D. Listing agreements

10. Which type of agent represents a buyer who asks for assistance finding a home?

    A. Presumed buyer's agent (no written agreement)

    B. Buyer's agent (by written agreement)

    C. Cooperating agent

    D. Dual agent

11. A broker acting as a dual agent appoints the intra-company agent for the

    A. Seller, and serves as the agent for the buyer

    B. Buyer, and serves as the agent for the seller

    C. Seller and buyer

    D. Commission

12. Before an agent presents an offer for a client,

    A. Presumed buyer agency must be terminated

    B. The agent and the buyer must enter into an oral brokerage agreement

    C. The right of first refusal must be offered

    D. There must be no outstanding offers

13. Fees are set by

    A.   Negotiation

    B.   The Real Estate Commission

    C.   The Local Association of Realtors

    D.   The National Association of Realtors

14. The licensee shall remain informed of matters
    affecting real estate in the

    A.   Block, county, and state

    B.   Block, continent, and world

    C.   State, nation, and world

    D.   Community, state, and nation

15. A broker wishing to provide evidence of reasonable
    and adequate supervision would produce evidence of

    A.   Scheduled open houses

    B.   Promotional material on website

    C.   Informing affiliates of new real estate laws

    D.   Equitable title

16. To prevent loss of license while awaiting an appeal, a licensee would need to post a bond not to exceed

    A. $15,000

    B. $25,000

    C. $30,000

    D. $50,000

17. Which type of agent represents the both the buyer and seller?

    A. Seller's agent

    B. Buyer's agent

    C. Dual agent

    D. Cooperating agent

18. Brokers are their clients'

    A. Principals

    B. Agents

    C. Attorneys

    D. Employees

19. Which applies to advertising in Maryland?

    A. Broker's name must be shown conspicuously with a phone number

    B. Licensee may use nickname rather than name as it appears on license in all advertising

    C. Cracked foundations must be disclosed in ads

    D. Ads should target ethnic groups

20. Which would the Commission consider an office?

    A. An answering service

    B. A mechanical recording device

    C. A mail drop

    D. Leasehold estate at will

21. A licensee shall keep copies of listings and other real estate documents for

    A. 3 years

    B. 5 years

    C. 7 years

    D. 9 years

22. A Team must consist of two or more Associate
Brokers or Salespersons or a combination whom

    A. Work together on an irregular basis

    B. Represent themselves as being separate entities

    C. Designate themselves by a collective name

    D. Restrict loans for an area

23. The Broker or Branch Office Manager

    A. Must supervise the Team Members in addition
to the supervision of the Team Leader

    B. May delegate their supervisory responsibilities
over Team Members to the Team Leader

    C. Need not use the equal housing disclosure

    D. Should disclose if the seller has AIDS

24. Fair Housing protected statuses in Maryland include

    A. Martial status and political party

    B. Sexual orientation and education level

    C. Martial status and sexual orientation

    D. Political party and education level

25. Which legal description is not recognized in
    Maryland?

    A. Lot and block

    B. Metes and bounds

    C. Government rectangular system

    D. Plat

26. Any ground lease holder must have registered that
    ground lease by September 30, 2010 or

    A. It is extinguished under the law

    B. Ground rent is doubled

    C. The tenant pays for taxes, repairs, and insurance

    D. The lease automatically renews

27. A right of cancellation is given to a purchaser of a
    resale timeshare or condominium for

    A. 7 days

    B. 10 days

    C. 15 days

    D. 30 days

28. A maximum interest rate of 24% applies in Maryland
to

   A. First mortgages

   B. Second mortgages

   C. Escrow accounts

   D. Security deposits

29. The Code of Ethics requires all of the following except

   A. Protect the public

   B. Protect the client

   C. Protect the Commissioners

   D. Avoid harm to a fellow licensee

30. Maryland's Statute of Frauds requires that

   A. No commission can be earned by an unlicensed
   individual

   B. Real estate licensees give legal advice

   C. Transfers of any interest in real property for more
   than one year must be in writing and signed

   D. Mortgage payments be level

Sample Exam 3 Answer Key

1. D

2. B

3. B

4. D

5. A

6. A

7. B

8. A

9. C

10. A

11. C

12. A

13. A

14. D

15. C

16. D

17. C

18. B

19. A

20. D

21. B

22. C

23. A

24. C

25. C

26. A

27. A

28. B

29. C

30. C

Sample Exam 3 with Answers Shown

1. The Maryland Real Estate Commission licensed
   commissioners must have been licensed for at least

   A. 4 years

   B. 5 years

   C. 7 years

   *D. 10 years

2. The minimum level of the Guaranty Fund is

   A. $25,000

   *B. $250,000

   C. $2,500,000

   D. $25,000,000

3. Time to respond to the Commission for a claim against
   the Guaranty Fund is

   A. 3 days

   *B. 10 days

   C. 20 days

   D. 30 days

4. Each Real Estate Hearing Board shall consist of at least three members of the Commission including

   A. The Chairperson

   B. The Executive Director

   C. At least two professional members

   *D. At least one professional member and at least one consumer member

5. A licensee may become affiliated with more than one broker

   *A. If each broker is given notice of the affiliations

   B. If one is outside the state

   C. With written permission from the Commission

   D. Under no circumstances

6. License renewal notices are mailed within

   *A. 30 days of expiration

   B. 3 months of expiration

   C. 6 months of expiration

   D. 1 year of expiration

7. How many of the continuing education hours must be on the topic of Legislative Updates?

A. 1.5 hours

*B. 3 hours

C. 7.5 hours

D. 9 hours

8. An unlicensed employee may

*A. Place signs on the property

B. Conduct an open house

C. Receive commission checks

D. Collect deposit monies

9. A broker wishing to provide evidence of reasonable and adequate supervision would produce evidence of

A. Commission checks

B. The broker's legal opinion on executed contracts

*C. Compliance with the firm's written procedures

D. Listing agreements

10. Which type of agent represents a buyer who asks for assistance finding a home?

    *A. Presumed buyer's agent (no written agreement)

    B.   Buyer's agent (by written agreement)

    C.   Cooperating agent

    D.   Dual agent

11. A broker acting as a dual agent appoints the intra-company agent for the

    A. Seller, and serves as the agent for the buyer

    B. Buyer, and serves as the agent for the seller

    *C. Seller and buyer

    D. Commission

12. Before an agent presents an offer for a client,

    *A. Presumed buyer agency must be terminated

    B. The agent and the buyer must enter into an oral brokerage agreement

    C. The right of first refusal must be offered

    D. There must be no outstanding offers

13. Fees are set by

    *A. Negotiation

    B.   The Real Estate Commission

    C.   The Local Association of Realtors

    D.   The National Association of Realtors

14. The licensee shall remain informed of matters affecting real estate in the

    A.   Block, county, and state

    B.   Block, continent, and world

    C.   State, nation, and world

    *D. Community, state, and nation

15. A broker wishing to provide evidence of reasonable and adequate supervision would produce evidence of

    A.   Scheduled open houses

    B.   Promotional material on website

    *C. Informing affiliates of new real estate laws

    D.   Equitable title

16. To prevent loss of license while awaiting an appeal, a
licensee would need to post a bond not to exceed

   A. $15,000

   B. $25,000

   C. $30,000

   *D. $50,000

17. Which type of agent represents the both the buyer
and seller?

   A. Seller's agent

   B. Buyer's agent

   *C. Dual agent

   D. Cooperating agent

18. Brokers are their clients'

   A. Principals

   *B. Agents

   C. Attorneys

   D. Employees

19. Which applies to advertising in Maryland?

    *A. Broker's name must be shown conspicuously with a phone number

    B. Licensee may use nickname rather than name as it appears on license in all advertising

    C. Cracked foundations must be disclosed in ads

    D. Ads should target ethnic groups

20. Which would the Commission consider an office?

    A. An answering service

    B. A mechanical recording device

    C. A mail drop

    *D. Leasehold estate at will

21. A licensee shall keep copies of listings and other real estate documents for

    A. 3 years

    *B. 5 years

    C. 7 years

    D. 9 years

.l

22. A Team must consist of two or more Associate Brokers or Salespersons or a combination whom

    A. Work together on an irregular basis

    B. Represent themselves as being separate entities

    *C. Designate themselves by a collective name

    D. Restrict loans for an area

23. The Broker or Branch Office Manager

    *A. Must supervise the Team Members in addition to the supervision of the Team Leader

    B. May delegate their supervisory responsibilities over Team Members to the Team Leader

    C. Need not use the equal housing disclosure

    D. Should disclose if the seller has AIDS

24. Fair Housing protected statuses in Maryland include

    A. Martial status and political party

    B. Sexual orientation and education level

    *C. Martial status and sexual orientation

    D. Political party and education level

25. Which legal description is not recognized in
Maryland?

   A. Lot and block

   B. Metes and bounds

   *C. Government rectangular system

   D. Plat

26. Any ground lease holder must have registered that
ground lease by September 30, 2010 or

   *A. It is extinguished under the law

   B. Ground rent is doubled

   C. The tenant pays for taxes, repairs, and insurance

   D. The lease automatically renews

27. A right of cancellation is given to a purchaser of a
resale timeshare or condominium for

   *A. 7 days

   B. 10 days

   C. 15 days

   D. 30 days

28. A maximum interest rate of 24% applies in Maryland to

    A. First mortgages

    *B. Second mortgages

    C. Escrow accounts

    D. Security deposits

29. The Code of Ethics requires all of the following except

    A. Protect the public

    B. Protect the client

    *C. Protect the Commissioners

    D. Avoid harm to a fellow licensee

30. Maryland's Statute of Frauds requires that

    A. No commission can be earned by an unlicensed individual

    B. Real estate licensees give legal advice

    *C. Transfers of any interest in real property for more than one year must be in writing and signed

    D. Mortgage payments be level

Sample Exam 4

1. The Real Estate Commission licensed commissioners must have lived in the area they represent for at least

   A. 3 years

   B. 4 years

   C. 5 years

   D. 10 years

2. Which is a power and duty of the Commission?

   A. To issue surety bonds

   B. To regulate appraisers

   C. To adopt a code of ethics

   D. To set maximum loan origination fees

3. Time a complainant has to request a payment from the Guaranty Fund is

   A. 90 days

   B. 1 year

   C. 3 years

   D. 7 years

4. What is the level of claim against the Guaranty Fund at
which the Commission may issue an order to pay or
deny the claim?

 A. $3,000

 B. $5,000

 C. $7,500

 D. $10,000

5. Licenses are granted for

 A. 2-year terms

 B. 3-year terms

 C. 4-year terms

 D. 5-year terms

6. To qualify for a salespersons license, an applicant shall
obtain

 A. Reciprocity

 B. Irrevocable consent

 C. An earnest money deposit

 D. A commitment to become affiliated with a broker

7. How many continuing education hours for residential
license renewal must be on the topic of Fair Housing?

    A.   1.5 hours

    B.   3 hours

    C.   7.5 hours

    D.   9 hours

8. For how long must a licensee keep Continuing
Education (CE) certificates?

    A.   2 years

    B.   3 years

    C.   5 years

    D.   7 years

9. A broker must surrender a license under the broker's
control to the Commission upon

    A.   The request of the licensee's spouse

    B.   The licensee's leave of absence

    C.   The license being suspended or revoked

    D.   The licensee's arrest for drunk driving

10. A salesperson offering to pay for new appliances for a buyer who purchases a home is an example of

A. Steering

B. Advertising

C. Misappropriation

D. An unfair inducement

11. Nonresidential property does not include

A. Commercial or industrial property

B. Unimproved property zoned for multifamily units

C. Property improved by five or more single-family units

D. Property zoned for agricultural use

12. Days notice needed for conversion to a condo are

A. 60 days

B. 90 days

C. 180 days

D. 270 days

13. Which is true regarding foreclosures?

    A. Lenders prefer judicial foreclosures

    B. Non-judicial foreclosures are associated with a power-of-sale clause

    C. Strict foreclosures are common in Maryland

    D. Acceleration is substituting a third party for a creditor

14. Licenses should refrain from disclosing knowledge of

    A. A property owner having AIDS

    B. Hidden defects

    C. Material defects

    D. Underground storage tanks

15. Upon the death of a broker, any family member may carry on the brokerage firm for up to

    A. 30 days

    B. 60 days

    C. 90 days

    D. 6 months

16. Which type of agent represents the seller and works for a different company than the seller's agent?

    A. Intra-company agent

    B. Cooperating agent

    C. Fiduciary

    D. Dual agent

17. An agent that negotiates on behalf of a buyer is a

    A. Presumed buyer's agent (no written agreement)

    B. Buyer's agent (by written agreement)

    C. Special agent

    D. Principal

18. Presumed agency ends upon

    A. An offer being discussed

    B. Showing a property listed with the licensee's own company

    C. An oral buyer agency agreement

    D. The substitution of a new contract

19. Which is not an undesirable business practice?

    A. Misleading advertising

    B. Blockbusting

    C. Prejudicial solicitation

    D. Referral fees

20. The requirement for an agent to maintain confidentiality could end as the result of

    A. The Statute of Limitations

    B. The expiration of the agency agreement

    C. The information becoming common knowledge from other sources

    D. An offer being withdrawn

21. A licensee changing ownership interest in a brokerage firm must notify the Commission within

    A. 30 days

    B. 60 days

    C. 6 months

    D. 1 year

22. Which is true regarding Teams or Groups?

    A. The team name in advertisements must be directly connected to the name of the brokerage

    B. A team may operate out of a location other than the office where their licenses are displayed

    C. Both parties agree to act in a unilateral contract

    D. Special agent teams may perform any and all acts

23. A Competitive Market Analysis (CMA)

    A. Is not an appraisal

    B. Requires an appraisal license for preparation

    C. Is most often used to value churches and libraries

    D. Is based on the capitalization of cash flows

24. The Commission may revoke the license of a licensee found guilty of any of the following except

    A. Bad faith

    B. Dishonesty

    C. Fraudulent dealings

    D. Reckless driving

25. The seller condition disclosure / disclaimer

    A. Should be completed by the intra-company agent at the time of listing

    B. Does not require the seller to disclose any latent defects known to them

    C. Should not have any blanks or missing items

    D. Must disclose if the seller has AIDS

26. Which legal description is most common in Maryland?

    A. Lot and block

    B. Metes and bounds

    C. Government rectangular system

    D. Homestead

27. Determination of whether or not a listed property carries a ground rent is

    A. The listing agent's responsibility

    B. The prospective buyer's responsibility

    C. The buyer's agent's responsibility

    D. Optional

28. Days notice needed for conversion to a timeshare are

    A. 30 days

    B. 60 days

    C. 90 days

    D. 120 days

29. Which is most accurate regarding a Deed of Trust?

    A. It contains no warranties or obligations

    B. It only allows for judicial foreclosure

    C. It contains a power-of-sale clause

    D. It returns the title to the trustor

30. Which is most accurate regarding the protection of
    the Chesapeake Bay?

    A. The Critical Area is within 1000 feet of the
        average high-water line

    B. The Buffer Zone is 1500 feet

    C. A 1980 law provided funds for cleanup

    D. The bay is protected by the Department of
        Transportation

Sample Exam 4 Answer Key

1. C

2. C

3. C

4. A

5. A

6. D

7. A

8. C

9. C

10. D

11. D

12. C

13. B

14. A

15. D

16. B

17. B

18. B

19. D

20. C

21. A

22. A

23. A

24. D

25. C

26. A

27. A

28. D

29. C

30. A

Sample Exam 4 with Answers Shown

1. The Real Estate Commission licensed commissioners
   must have lived in the area they represent for at least

   A. 3 years

   B. 4 years

   *C. 5 years

   D. 10 years

2. Which is a power and duty of the Commission?

   A. To issue surety bonds

   B. To regulate appraisers

   *C. To adopt a code of ethics

   D. To set maximum loan origination fees

3. Time a complainant has to request a payment from the
   Guaranty Fund is

   A. 90 days

   B. 1 year

   *C. 3 years

   D. 7 years

4. What is the level of claim against the Guaranty Fund at which the Commission may issue an order to pay or deny the claim?

　*A. $3,000

　B.　$5,000

　C.　$7,500

　D.　$10,000

5. Licenses are granted for

　*A. 2-year terms

　B.　3-year terms

　C.　4-year terms

　D.　5-year terms

6. To qualify for a salespersons license, an applicant shall obtain

　A.　Reciprocity

　B.　Irrevocable consent

　C.　An earnest money deposit

　*D. A commitment to become affiliated with a broker

7. How many continuing education hours for residential license renewal must be on the topic of Fair Housing?

   *A. 1.5 hours

   B.   3 hours

   C.   7.5 hours

   D.   9 hours

8. For how long must a licensee keep Continuing Education (CE) certificates?

   A.   2 years

   B.   3 years

   *C. 5 years

   D.   7 years

9. A broker must surrender a license under the broker's control to the Commission upon

   A.   The request of the licensee's spouse

   B.   The licensee's leave of absence

   *C. The license being suspended or revoked

   D.   The licensee's arrest for drunk driving

10. A salesperson offering to pay for new appliances for a
buyer who purchases a home is an example of

    A. Steering

    B. Advertising

    C. Misappropriation

    *D. An unfair inducement

11. Nonresidential property does not include

    A. Commercial or industrial property

    B. Unimproved property zoned for multifamily units

    C. Property improved by five or more single-family
units

    *D. Property zoned for agricultural use

12. Days notice needed for conversion to a condo are

    A. 60 days

    B. 90 days

    *C. 180 days

    D. 270 days

13. Which is true regarding foreclosures?

    A. Lenders prefer judicial foreclosures

    *B. Non-judicial foreclosures are associated with a power-of-sale clause

    C. Strict foreclosures are common in Maryland

    D. Acceleration is substituting a third party for a creditor

14. Licenses should refrain from disclosing knowledge of

    *A. A property owner having AIDS

    B. Hidden defects

    C. Material defects

    D. Underground storage tanks

15. Upon the death of a broker, any family member may carry on the brokerage firm for up to

    A. 30 days

    B. 60 days

    C. 90 days

    *D. 6 months

16. Which type of agent represents the seller and works for a different company than the seller's agent?

    A. Intra-company agent

    *B. Cooperating agent

    C. Fiduciary

    D. Dual agent

17. An agent that negotiates on behalf of a buyer is a

    A. Presumed buyer's agent (no written agreement)

    *B. Buyer's agent (by written agreement)

    C. Special agent

    D. Principal

18. Presumed agency ends upon

    A. An offer being discussed

    *B. Showing a property listed with the licensee's own company

    C. An oral buyer agency agreement

    D. The substitution of a new contract

19. Which is not an undesirable business practice?

    A. Misleading advertising

    B. Blockbusting

    C. Prejudicial solicitation

    *D. Referral fees

20. The requirement for an agent to maintain confidentiality could end as the result of

    A. The Statute of Limitations

    B. The expiration of the agency agreement

    *C. The information becoming common knowledge from other sources

    D. An offer being withdrawn

21. A licensee changing ownership interest in a brokerage firm must notify the Commission within

    *A. 30 days

    B. 60 days

    C. 6 months

    D. 1 year

22. Which is true regarding Teams or Groups?

   *A. The team name in advertisements must be directly connected to the name of the brokerage

   B. A team may operate out of a location other than the office where their licenses are displayed

   C. Both parties agree to act in a unilateral contract

   D. Special agent teams may perform any and all acts

23. A Competitive Market Analysis (CMA)

   *A. Is not an appraisal

   B. Requires an appraisal license for preparation

   C. Is most often used to value churches and libraries

   D. Is based on the capitalization of cash flows

24. The Commission may revoke the license of a licensee found guilty of any of the following except

   A. Bad faith

   B. Dishonesty

   C. Fraudulent dealings

   *D. Reckless driving

25. The seller condition disclosure / disclaimer

    A. Should be completed by the intra-company agent
        at the time of listing

    B. Does not require the seller to disclose any latent
        defects known to them

    *C. Should not have any blanks or missing items

    D. Must disclose if the seller has AIDS

26. Which legal description is most common in Maryland?

    *A. Lot and block

    B. Metes and bounds

    C. Government rectangular system

    D. Homestead

27. Determination of whether or not a listed property
    carries a ground rent is

    *A. The listing agent's responsibility

    B. The prospective buyer's responsibility

    C. The buyer's agent's responsibility

    D. Optional

28. Days notice needed for conversion to a timeshare are

    A. 30 days

    B. 60 days

    C. 90 days

    *D. 120 days

29. Which is most accurate regarding a Deed of Trust?

    A. It contains no warranties or obligations

    B. It only allows for judicial foreclosure

    *C. It contains a power-of-sale clause

    D. It returns the title to the trustor

30. Which is most accurate regarding the protection of the Chesapeake Bay?

    *A. The Critical Area is within 1000 feet of the average high-water line

    B. The Buffer Zone is 1500 feet

    C. A 1980 law provided funds for cleanup

    D. The bay is protected by the Department of Transportation

Duties and Powers of the Commission

General Powers

The Maryland Real Estate Commission:

- Five (5) licensed (professional) members and four (4) unlicensed (consumer) members

- Licensed commissioners must have been licensed for at least ten (10) years and have lived in the area they represent for at least five (5) years

- Staff employees include the Executive Director, Education Administrator, and Investigators

Powers and Duties of the Maryland Real Estate Commission:

- To issue, deny, suspend, and revoke licenses

- To take action against unlicensed individuals

- To amend, adopt, and repeal rules and regulations

- To adopt a code of ethics

Duties and Powers of the Commission

General Powers (continued)

Fees and funds collected by the Commission:

- Placed in the General Fund

- Set in statute

- Can be amended by the General Assembly

Prior to making changes to rules and regulations, the Maryland Real Estate Commission must post the proposed changes on the Maryland Register for 45 days

Maryland Real Estate Commission's website:

- Links to real estate laws

- License requirements

- List of approved education providers

Duties and Powers of the Commission

Investigations, Hearings, and Appeals

Prior to taking action the Maryland Real Estate
Commission must hold a hearing

Prior to a hearing, a licensee being investigated gets at
least 10 days notice

The time to respond to the Commission concerning a
written inquiry is 20 days

Each Real Estate Hearing Board shall consist of at least
three members of the Commission including at least
one professional member and at least one consumer
member

To prevent loss of license while awaiting an appeal, a
licensee would need to post a bond not to exceed
$50,000

Duties and Powers of the Commission

Suspensions, Revocations, and Fines

The Commission may revoke the license of a licensee
found guilty of bad faith, dishonesty, or fraudulent
dealings (not necessarily for a driving under the
influence conviction)

Maximum fine that the Maryland Real Estate Commission
is authorized to impose: $5,000 for the first violation,
$15,000 for the second, and $25,000 for the third

Examples of Disciplinary actions:

- Revocation and fine - Theft conviction; Sending
  false and misleading notices; Forging signatures;
  Dishonest and fraudulent dealings

- Suspension and fine - Failing to disclose an
  easement; Misrepresentation

- Consent order and agreement - Failing to provide
  evidence of continuing education

- Reprimand - Failing to return phone calls in a
  timely manner

- Application denied - Applicant with convictions
  on financial matters involving trust

Duties and Powers of the Commission

Guaranty Fund

Guaranty fund award: Compensates a third party as a result of misconduct of a licensee

Amount each licensee initially pays into the Guaranty Fund: $20

Minimum level required to be maintained by the Guaranty Fund: $250,000

Time to respond to the Commission for a claim against the Guaranty Fund is 10 days

Time a complainant has to request a payment from the Guaranty Fund is 3 years

Maximum penalty for a false claim: $5,000 and/or 1 year

Claims for payments from the Guaranty Fund:

- Are required to be in writing

- Must be for actual cash loss due to actions of a licensee

- May not be filed by the spouse of the individual responsible for the act

- Maximum amount that can be recovered is $25,000

- Licensee's license is suspended after payment

Licensing Requirements

Activities Requiring a License

Persons who must conform to Brokers Act but are not required to hold licenses:

- Financial institutions leasing or selling foreclosures

- Lawyers not regularly engaged in real estate brokerage services

- Homebuilders in the initial rental and sale of new homes

- Agents of brokers or owners of real estate while managing or leasing that real estate

- Persons who negotiate business leases

- Owners who subdivide not more than six unimproved lots

Licensing Requirements

Activities Requiring a License (continued)

An unlicensed employee may

- Answer the telephone and forward calls to the licensee

- Submit changes and listings to a multiple listing service

- Follow-up on loan commitments after a contract has been signed

- Assemble documents for closing

- Secure documents from courthouse and public utilities

- Have keys made for company listings

- Place signs on the property

- Schedule an open house

- Compute commission checks

Licensing Requirements

Activities Requiring a License (continued)

An unlicensed employee may not:

- Show property

- Answer any questions on listings, title, financing, or closing

- Prepare promotional material or ads without the review and approval of the licensee and supervising broker

- Discuss or explain a contract, listing, or lease with anyone outside the brokerage

- Be paid on the basis of real estate activity

- Discuss the attributes or amenities of a property with a prospective purchaser or lessee

- Collect or hold deposit money or rent

Licensing Requirements

Initial Licenses

Licenses are granted for 2-year terms

Classroom hours required for an initial salesperson
license: 60 hours

To qualify for a salespersons license, an applicant shall
obtain a commitment to become affiliated with a
broker

A salesperson can be affiliated with more than one
broker if each broker is given notice of the affiliations

To be licensed, applicants must be professionally
competent and of good character and reputation

Licensing Requirements

Initial Licenses (continued)

To qualify for a broker's license, an applicant needs to:

- Complete 135 hours of required education

- Have three years of experience as a salesperson

- Submit a credit report to the commission

Classroom hours on Ethics required for an initial broker's license: 3 hours

A waiver of requirements may be given to a licensee holding a license in another state if Maryland and that state have reciprocity

States with reciprocity with Maryland as of 2010: Oklahoma and Pennsylvania

If an individual wishes to be licensed in Maryland and lives in another state, the individual would need to submit irrevocable consent

Licensing Requirements

Change in License Status and Renewals

A license may be placed on inactive status for up to 4 years

Expired licenses may be reinstated within 4 years of expiration

License renewal notices are mailed within 30 days of expiration – the licensee is responsible for renewal

The licensee shall remain informed of matters affecting real estate in the community, state, and nation

Continuing education is completed during the term of the license and prior to submitting a renewal application

How long must a licensee keep Continuing Education (CE) certificates: 5 years

Not more than three hours of the continuing education requirement may be on the topic of Technology

Licensing Requirements

Continuing Education Requirements

Continuing education hours required for residential and commercial license renewal: 15 hours (7.5 hours for licensees with a law degree)

Mandatory continuing education topics required for residential license renewal:

- Legislative Update (3 hours)

- Fair Housing (1.5 hours, residential only)

- Ethics, Flipping and Predatory Lending (3 hours)

After January 1, 2012, continuing education must include:

- At least three hours every four years on Agency and Agency Disclosure

- For brokers, branch managers, and team leaders; at least three hours every four years on Broker Supervision

- At least 10.5 hours from required subject matter

Licensing Requirements

Broker's Place of Business

Prior to changing the location of an office or escrow account, a broker must give the Commission 7 days notice

Automatic suspension of a broker's license could occur for:

- Failing to provide notice of address change

- Failing to provide upon request all records concerning earnest money deposits

Upon the death of a broker, any family member may carry on the brokerage firm for up to 6 months

Salespersons and associate brokers licenses must be displayed in the broker's branch office

A licensee acquiring or disposing of an ownership interest in a firm providing brokerage services must notify the Commission within 30 days

Licensing Requirements

Broker's Place of Business (continued)

The Commission would not consider an office:

- An answering service

- A mechanical recording device

- A mail drop

A broker must surrender a license under the broker's control to the Commission upon:

- The request of the licensee

- The licensee's death

- A finding from the Commission that the license should be suspended or revoked

Maximum any salesperson or associate broker can hold including family holdings: 50% interest

Business Conduct

Listing Agreements and Offers

Illegal practices in Maryland:

- Net listings

- Automatic extensions

Licensee must give copies to each party in a timely
manner and keep a copy for the licensee's records

All agreements should be put in writing

A Competitive Market Analysis (CMA) is not an appraisal
– it is intended only for assisting in deciding the buying,
offering, or sale price of real property

All written offers must be presented in a timely manner

If an additional offer comes in while a property is under
contract, it must be presented in a timely manner

Business Conduct

Listing Agreements and Offers (continued)

Maryland's Statute of Frauds requires that transfers of
any interest in real property for more than one year
must be in writing and signed

Buyer has the right to choose the buyer's settlement
attorney, escrow agent, and title company

Title insurance in Maryland: State law requires that
purchasers be offered homeowner's title insurance at
closing

A buyer is responsible for securing evidence of title in
Maryland

Listing contracts are with brokers not with the
salesperson

If a salesperson leaves a brokerage, the listings stay with
the brokerage

Business Conduct

Disclosure of Agency

The Brokers Act requires that the form Understanding Whom Agents Represent be presented not later than the first scheduled face-to-face meeting

Agents that represents the seller:

- Seller's agent

- Cooperating agent – works for a different company than the seller's agent

Agents that represents the buyer:

- Presumed buyer's agent (no written agreement) - represents a buyer who asks for assistance

- Buyer's agent (by written agreement) - negotiates on behalf of a buyer

A broker acting as a dual agent representing both the buyer and the seller appoints a seller's intra-company agent and a buyer's intra-company agent

Only the Broker may designate Team Members as intra-company agents

Business Conduct

Disclosure of Agency (continued)

A customer could infer that an agency relationship exists based on receipt of magisterial (expert) guidance

Unless a property is listed by an agent or the agent's broker, an agent is assumed to be buyer's agent

Before an agent negotiates a purchase or presents an offer on behalf of a client; presumed buyer agency must be terminated, and the agent and the buyer must enter into a written brokerage agreement

Presumed agency ends upon:

- An offer being written

- Showing a property listed with the licensee's own company

- A signed buyer agency agreement or rejecting representation

Broker's clients are their principals and brokers are their clients' agents; agents owe clients fiduciary duties of care, obedience, loyalty, disclosure, accounting, and confidentiality

Agency can end by mutual agreement

Business Conduct

Disclosures

When selling or leasing a property in which the licensee has an ownership interest, the licensee must reveal the interest in writing to all parties in the transaction, with the exception of short-term leases

Licensees must gather material facts by:

- Checking public records

- Having the seller complete disclosure forms

- Inspecting the property and reviewing the survey

The seller condition disclosure / disclaimer:

- Should be completed by the seller at the time of listing

- Requires the seller to disclose any latent defects known to them

- Should not have any blanks or missing items

Business Conduct

Disclosures (continued)

The buyer has the right to void a sale if they did not sign off on the seller condition disclosure / disclaimer form prior to the sales contract; and the lender must disclose to the borrower the loss of the right at loan application to void the contract if the disclosure / disclaimer is not received

The requirement for agents to maintain confidentiality ends by permission from the client or the information becoming common knowledge from other sources

Licenses should refrain from disclosing knowledge of a property owner having AIDS

Stigmatized properties: The occurrence of a death or felony on a property is not a material fact that licensees are required to disclose

Not

Business Conduct

Disclosures (continued)

Determination of whether or not a listed property carries
a ground rent is the listing agent's responsibility

Any ground lease holder must have registered that
ground lease with the Maryland Department of
Assessments and Taxation by September 30, 2010 or it
is extinguished under the law and ground rent is no
longer payable

If a homeowner wants to buy a ground lease, the
purchase price is determined by dividing the annual
rent by a factor in the range of 0.04 to 0.12

A licensee may not post a sign or ad on which the cost
and capitalization of ground rent on the property is
shown in print that is smaller than the size of the print
used to show the price of the property

Business Conduct

Recordkeeping and Commissions

Client's money must be deposited by the broker or the
broker's designee in the firm's trust account (a demand
account such as a checking or savings account) within 7
business days, and records of trust money must be kept
in a secure area of the office

A licensee shall keep copies of listings and other real
estate documents for 5 years

The amount of brokerage agreed upon may be a specific
amount or a specific percentage

Fees are set by negotiation.

Referral fees may not be paid to unlicensed persons.

Based on the activity of a person who should have been
properly licensed but was not, a firm can claim no
commission

A broker may not pay a commission to an unlicensed
person: an exception is a broker licensed in another
state

Business Conduct

Advertising and Signs

Advertising in Maryland:

- Broker's name must be shown conspicuously with a phone number

- Licensee must use name as it appears on license in all advertising

All Team advertising must contain:

- The name of at least one licensee Team member

- The telephone number of the broker or the branch office manager

- The full name of the brokerage displayed in a meaningful and conspicuous manner

Callers exempt from calling numbers on the National Do Not Call Registry include charities, surveys, political organizations, and companies with which the recipient has done business with in the last 18 months

The Junk Fax Prevention Act allows unsolicited fax advertising if the sender has an established business relationship with the recipient, and the recipient has given permission to use the fax number

Business Conduct

Ethics

The Maryland Real Estate Commission's Code of Ethics
and the National Association of Realtors' Code of
Ethics are complementary in that neither contradicts
the other

The Maryland Real Estate Commission's Code of Ethics
can be found in the COMAR

The Code of Ethics requires that licensees

- Protect the public

- Protect the client

- Not interfere with the exclusive listing of a
  competitor, so as to avoid harm to a fellow
  licensee

A salesperson offering to pay for new appliances for a
buyer who purchases a home is an example of an
unfair inducement

A licensee may not place a "for sale" sign on a property
without the owner's permission

Business Conduct

Fair Housing Laws and Regulations

Fair Housing protected statuses in Maryland:

- Martial status

- Sexual orientation

Listed in the Maryland regulations as undesirable practices:

- Misleading advertising

- Exploitation, blockbusting, and steering

- Prejudicial solicitation and discriminatory practices

Business Conduct

Supervision Requirements

A broker wishing to provide evidence of reasonable and adequate supervision would produce evidence of

- Review of all executed contracts

- Affiliates' attendance at sales and training meetings

- Review of all advertisements placed by affiliate

- Compliance with the firm's written procedures and policies distributed to affiliates

- Procedures for informing affiliates of new or changed real estate laws and regulations

Team Leaders must:

- Have at least three years experience

- Exercise reasonable and adequate supervision over the provision of real estate services by members of the team

- Maintain a current list of all team members and employees and provide the list to the broker or branch office manager where the Team Members' licenses are displayed

Business Conduct

Supervision Requirements (continued)

The Broker or Branch Office Manager must supervise the
Team Members, and this supervision is in addition to
the supervision of the Team Leader

Teams and Groups:

- A licensed broker may not be a member of a
Team

- The team name may not contain the terms "Real
Estate", "Real Estate brokerage", or "Realty"

- Team members must conduct all real estate
brokerage activities from the office where their
license are displayed

A Team must consist of two or more Associate Brokers or
Salespersons or a combination of the two whom:

- Work together on a regular basis

- Represent themselves to the public as being part
of one entity

- Designate themselves by a collective name such
as Team or Group

Business Conduct

Knowledge of Other Maryland State Laws

Legal descriptions in Maryland:

- Lot and block (plat) - Most common

- Metes and bounds - Outlines property and uses a point of beginning (POB)

- Government rectangular system - Not recognized

Legal life estates not recognized in Maryland: Curtesy, Dower, or Homestead

Nonresidential property includes

- Commercial or industrial property

- Unimproved property zoned for multifamily units

- Property improved by five or more single-family units

Nonresidential property does not include property zoned for agricultural use

Business Conduct

Knowledge of Other Maryland State Laws (continued)

Right of cancellation given to purchaser:

- New timeshare - 10 days

- New condominium - 15 days

- Resale timeshare or condominium - 7 days

Days notice needed for conversion:

- Timeshare - 120 days

- Condo - 180 days

Deed of Trust

- Security instrument preferred by Maryland lenders

- Contains a power-of-sale clause

- Allows for non-judicial foreclosure

Usary: A maximum interest rate of 24% applies in Maryland to second mortgages

Business Conduct

Knowledge of Other Maryland State Laws (continued)

Security deposits in Maryland:

- Maximum 2 months rent

- Interest on security deposits accrues every six months and does not compound

- If there are no damages, security deposits must be returned with interest within 45 days

Leases in Maryland:

- Maximum late penalty 5%

- May not include automatic renewal for longer than one month

- May include covenant for the tenant to restore the premises in good repair

In Maryland, only a legally married couple can own property as tenant by the entirety; the survivor upon death holds the property in severalty

Business Conduct

Knowledge of Other Maryland State Laws (continued)

Fire protection systems in Maryland:

- Sprinkler systems must be installed in every newly constructed dormitory, hotel, lodging or rooming house, town house, and multifamily residential dwelling

- At least one smoke detector must be installed on each level of every newly constructed dwelling units, including basements, excluding attics

The Chesapeake Bay Critical Area is within 1000 feet of the average high-water line

Maryland Lead Poisoning Prevention Program:

- Participation is mandatory for all units built before 1950

- The program provides for reimbursements for up to $9,500 for relocation and $7,500 for medical expenses for children and pregnant women

Reference List

Annotated Code of Maryland and the Code of Maryland Regulations, 2010.

Coldwell Banker Residential Brokerage School of Real Estate, 2010.

Gaddy, Wade E. and Hart, Robert E. *Real Estate Fundamentals*, 7th Edition, 2007.

Galaty, Fillmore; Allaway, Wellington; and Kyle, Robert. *Modern Real Estate Practice*, 18th Edition, 2010.

Maryland Real Estate Commission Laws, Rules, and Regulations, 2010.

McCaulay, Philip Martin. *Real Estate Salesperson Licensing Exams and Study Guide*, 1st edition, 2007.

White, Donald. *Maryland Real Estate Practice and Law*, 12th Edition, 2008.

About the Author

Philip Martin McCaulay is an actuary with a degree in mathematics from Indiana University. He graduated from the Coldwell Banker Residential Brokerage School of Real Estate in Columbia, Maryland in 2010. He has sold thousands of study guides and practice exam books in the fields of pensions, investments, finance, real estate, and massage therapy. He has also published books on card games, cooking, and military history. He volunteers to write, publish, and ship free copies of books to troops through Operation Paperback.

1. A. B. C. D.	16. A. B. C. D.
2. A. B. C. D.	17. A. B. C. D.
3. A. B. C. D.	18. A. B. C. D.
4. A. B. C. D.	19. A. B. C. D.
5. A. B. C. D.	20. A. B. C. D.
6. A. B. C. D.	21. A. B. C. D.
7. A. B. C. D.	22. A. B. C. D.
8. A. B. C. D.	23. A. B. C. D.
9. A. B. C. D.	24. A. B. C. D.
10. A. B. C. D.	25. A. B. C. D.
11. A. B. C. D.	26. A. B. C. D.
12. A. B. C. D.	27. A. B. C. D.
13. A. B. C. D.	28. A. B. C. D.
14. A. B. C. D.	29. A. B. C. D.
15. A. B. C. D.	30. A. B. C. D.

Made in the USA
Lexington, KY
04 February 2012